PLANTING
THE SEED

A Guide to Gardening

BY SUZANNE WINCKLER

Lerner Publications Company · Minneapolis

This book is available in two editions:
Library binding by Lerner Publications Company, a division of Lerner Publishing Group
Soft cover by First Avenue Editions, an imprint of Lerner Publishing Group
241 First Avenue North
Minneapolis, MN 55401 U.S.A.

Website address: www.lernerbooks.com

Library of Congress Cataloging-in-Publication Data

Winckler, Suzanne, 1946–
    Planting the seed : a guide to gardening / by Suzanne Winckler.
       p.   cm.
    Includes bibliographical references and index.
    ISBN: 0–8225–0081–7 (lib. bdg. : alk. paper)
    ISBN: 0–8225–0471–5 (pbk. : alk. paper)
    1. Gardening—Juvenile literature. [1. Organic gardening.
    2. Gardening.] I. Title.
    SB457.W62 2002
    635'.0484—dc21   2001002018

Manufactured in the United States of America
1 2 3 4 5 6 – JR – 07 06 05 04 03 02

Table of
CONTENTS

INTRO

Take a trip to your local grocery store. Most likely you'll find fruits and vegetables of all kinds available any time of the year. With all of these foods readily available, why would people go to all the trouble to garden? Some people enjoy the challenge of gardening and growing their own food. Many gardeners like to know exactly where their food comes from and how it was grown. Unless a fruit or vegetable in the grocery store is identified as organically grown, there's a good chance that farmers used chemicals or pesticides during the growing process. By growing their own food, gardeners can be sure that the

DUCTION

fruits and vegetables they harvest are chemical and pesticide free. Plus, they are as fresh as they can be. Gardeners also value making the earth a better place to live. By conserving water, using no (or nontoxic) chemicals, and improving the soil, gardeners are protecting the environment in their own backyards. At the same time, they are putting nature's living things to work to grow food and flowers. This is called organic gardening.

The activities included in this book abide by the earth-friendly rules of organic gardening, suggesting alternatives to pesticides and chemicals and ways to enrich the soil naturally. If you have any questions as you garden, look for books or websites on organic gardening. Lists of resources are provided in the back of this book. Wondering what to do with the fruits of your labor? Check the harvest chapter for recipes. Most important, dig in, get your hands dirty, and have fun!

CHAPTER 1

THE BIG PICTURE

All plants need three basic things—sunlight, water, and soil. But the exact amounts of these differ for specific plants. For example, tomatoes thrive in sunny, hot places with lots of water. Broccoli and brussels sprouts like sun and water, too, but prefer cooler days and nights. Think about the climate where you live. How hot or cold does it get? How much rain falls in the summer? How many days does the sun shine? Also consider the soil in your garden. Is it sandy, or wet and sticky like clay? Gardeners must take all of these things into account when they decide what to grow.

FIND YOUR PLACE IN THE SUN

Just like the human body converts food into the energy it needs to function and grow, plants soak up sunlight and use it to make the chemical energy necessary to sprout and flourish. This process is called photosynthesis, and it is important to all living things on the earth. When we eat plants, we use that stored energy to fuel our bodies. You might say that when you eat green beans or broccoli from your garden, you are really eating sunlight.

The sun's intensity, or strength, is not the same all over the planet. Think of the earth as a spinning top. It spins on its axis, the imaginary rod running through the planet from the North Pole to the

South Pole. As the earth spins on its axis, it also orbits the sun. The rotation of the earth causes the top and bottom of the planet, or the North Pole and South Pole, to be close to the sun at certain times of the year and farther away from the sun at other times. This tilt of the earth on its axis is what gives us winter, spring, summer, and fall. If you live near the earth's equator, you don't have four seasons. Here, the planet always stays about the same distance from the sun. Sunshine in Ecuador is very different from sunshine in Iceland. And so is gardening in these two places!

Mapmakers measure distances and exact locations on the earth by dividing the planet into a grid system. Similar to the streets and avenues in a city, this grid is made up of the lines of longitude and latitude. Look at a globe or a world map. Longitude lines run from pole to pole. They measure distance from east to west. Latitude lines circle the globe perpendicular to the lines of longitude. They measure distances south and north of the equator.

Of these two measures, latitude is more important in

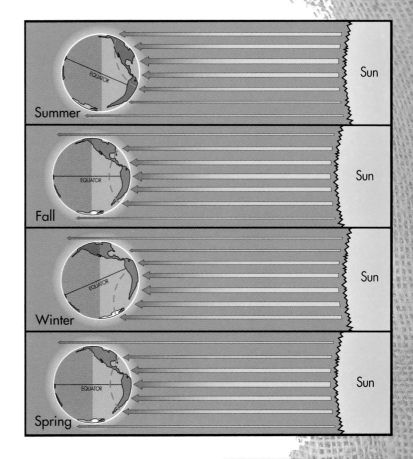

planning a garden. Can you figure out why? It relates to how the earth tilts on its axis. If your garden is at the equator—which is 0° latitude—you will have about the same amount of sun every day of the year. The higher your latitude, the less sunshine your plants will have between spring and fall. Places north of the equator have shorter growing seasons. For example, if you live in the small town of Grand Rapids, Minnesota, your latitude

In this drawing, the four seasons are shown as they happen in North America. When the sun directly hits North America, the continent experiences summer. As the earth tilts, the sun's heat is aimed elsewhere, and North America experiences the rest of the seasons.

is about 47° north of the equator. Your growing season is short. You will have trouble growing corn! Most varieties need seventy to eighty days to mature.

Locate your city or town on a country map. Write down the latitude and longitude where you live. This is your address on the earth. You'll need this information to select the plants that will grow best in your garden.

Climate Questions?

Answers to your climate questions are everywhere. Your county extension office can help. Many of these offices are on the Internet. Follow weather reports in the newspaper, on television, over the Internet, or on a weather radio station that broadcasts reports from the National Oceanic and Atmospheric Administration (NOAA). Keep a daily record of high and low temperatures, sunrise, sunset, and precipitation. Observation is the best way to learn about your climate.

RAINFALL AND OTHER CLIMATE CLUES

Climate is as important as location when deciding what to plant in your garden. Temperature, rainfall, and wind all combine to make up a region's climate. One tool gardeners rely on is the U.S. Department of Agriculture's Hardiness Zone map, which shows the lowest winter temperatures across the United States. The map divides the country into eleven zones. Zone 1 is a deep freeze in winter, with temperatures of −50°F (−10°C) or lower. Zone 11 is very balmy; winter temperatures never get below 40°F (4°C). Most seed catalogs, nurseries, and garden books tell you the hardiness zone for each plant. If a plant is hardy to Zone 8, and you live in Zone 5, you and the plant are not meant for each other. Consider, too, the amount of rain or snow that falls each year. Some plants thrive in humid regions where lots of rain falls. Others prefer the dry, desert conditions of the southwestern United States.

Once you know your hardiness zone and basic details about your climate, you can pick the right plants to grow in your garden. You may be tempted to grow a vegetable or flower just because you like it. Instead, remember this simple garden rule: every plant is adapted to a particular climate. Forcing a plant to grow where it does not belong is like making penguins live in a tropical rain forest.

DIG YOUR HANDS IN THE DIRT

Gardeners love to hold soil in their hands. By doing this, they can tell if the soil will hold the air, water, and nutrients that plants need to convert sunlight into energy. Soil comes in three basic types: sand, silt, and clay.

Sand

Have you ever picked up a handful of sand on a beach? Sand is composed of big particles of dirt you can see. The gritty, loose bits of sand easily slip through your fingers. These particles are too big to cling together. Sand is like a sieve. Water drains quickly in and around the particles. That's bad news for gardeners. It means there is no water to carry nutrients up from the soil to nourish your plants.

Getting your hands full of dirt will tell you a lot about your soil. Does it have worms in it? Does it crumble? Does it slide through your fingers or stick to them?

Silt and Clay

Silt is made of very small particles. You need a microscope to see them. Clay soil has even smaller particles. To see them you need an electron microscope. Water can barely squeeze through the tiny, tightly packed particles of silt and clay. There is hardly any room for air. When silt and clay soils get waterlogged, most plants die because they need air to survive.

HARDINESS ZONES

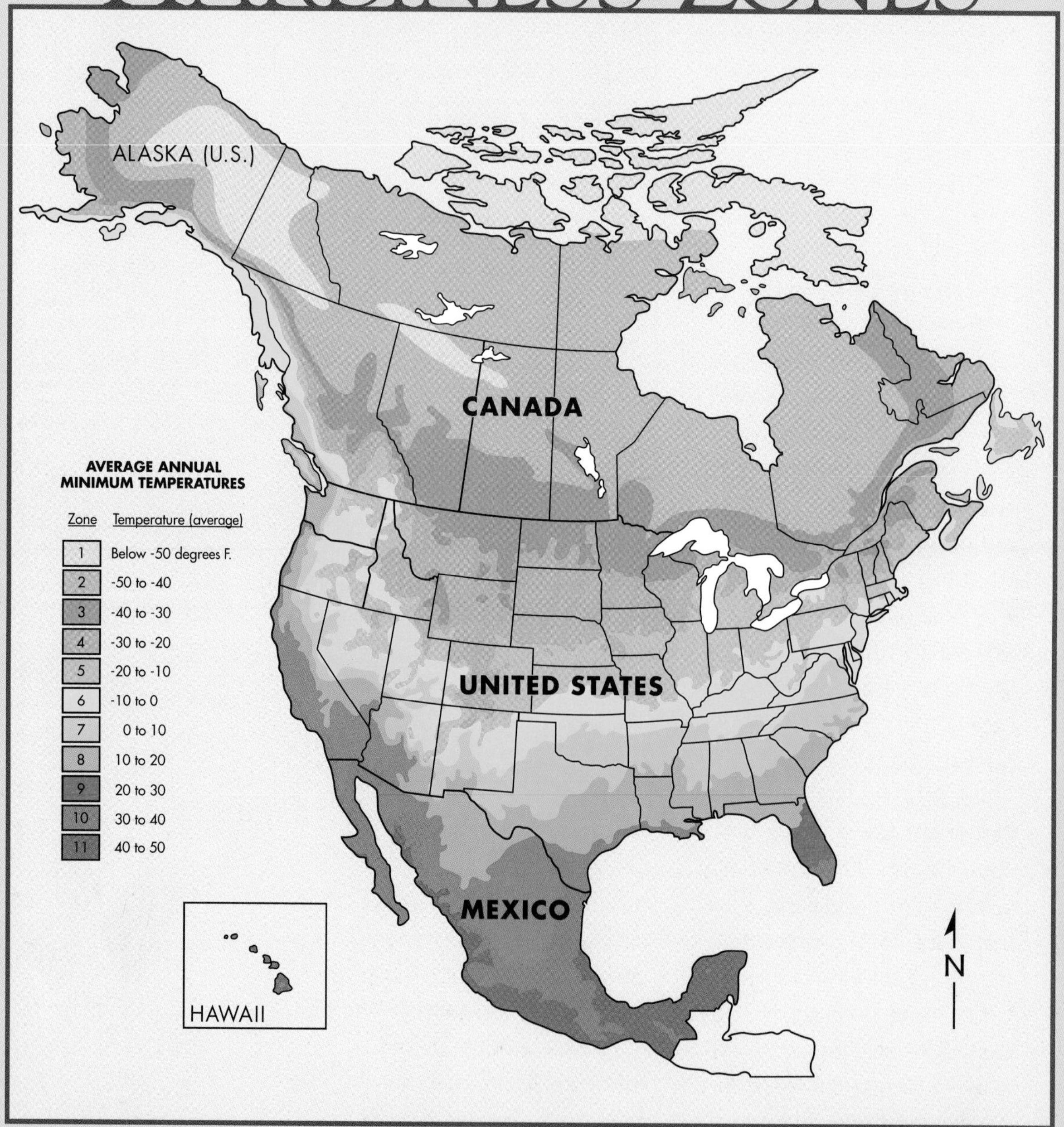

ALASKA (U.S.)

CANADA

**AVERAGE ANNUAL
MINIMUM TEMPERATURES**

Zone	Temperature (average)
1	Below -50 degrees F.
2	-50 to -40
3	-40 to -30
4	-30 to -20
5	-20 to -10
6	-10 to 0
7	0 to 10
8	10 to 20
9	20 to 30
10	30 to 40
11	40 to 50

UNITED STATES

MEXICO

HAWAII

N

Fortunately, most of the earth's soils are a mishmash of the three types. The best mix for gardening is loam, which is a blend of about 40 percent sand, 40 percent silt, and 20 percent clay. Unless you are very, very lucky, you will not find such perfect soil in your backyard. Don't worry. As long as you do not pick a sand dune or a bed of pure clay as your garden site, you can improve your soil by adding organic matter.

Organic matter used in gardening is simply any plant, whether alive or dead. When you give your garden soil regular feedings of organic matter, you add nutrients. You help create spaces in the soil where water and air can circulate. Organic matter also contains or attracts billions of creatures, such as bacteria and earthworms, that maintain the soil's health.

The chemistry of your soil is also important. Plants can't chew like we can. They "eat" by absorbing nutrients through their roots. These nutrients must be dissolved in water. Certain plants, such as blueberries, are adapted to "eat" nutrients dissolved in water that is acidic (like lemon juice).

Other plants, like sweet clover, prefer to have their "food" dissolved in a liquid that is alkaline (like baking soda mixed with water). Most plants like a soup that is not too acidic or too alkaline. To find out if the soil is acidic, alkaline, or neutral, gardeners test it for potential hydrogen—pH for short. Potential hydrogen measures the hydrogen ions in the soil. An ion is an atom or molecule with a positive or negative electric charge. The number of hydrogen ions determines how nutrients get absorbed. You can get a kit or meter to check your soil pH from many garden supply stores or nurseries. If your soil pH is between 6 and 7, it is in the neutral zone. Neutral pH is best for most gardens.

PICK YOUR GARDEN SPOT

When deciding where to plant your garden, it's most important to select a place with lots of sunshine. Remember, you are harnessing the sun's energy to fuel plants to grow big, plump fruits or vegetables for you. Your backyard is probably shaded part of the day by a tree, by shrubs, or by your house or

garage. Your job is to find the sunniest spot. A good place to start is on the south side of your house or apartment building. This part of your yard is most likely to be bathed in warm sunlight for most of the day. Once you've picked a spot, spend a day watching how sunlight travels over your garden. Unless you live near the equator, where the amount of sunshine remains pretty much the same throughout the year, you also have to think about how the seasons affect light. As spring changes to summer, the sun appears higher in the sky and the days get longer. Your garden will get more sunlight, and the shade patterns will shift. You will want to make a sun map in early May and another one in early July. Of course, by July your garden will already be planted, but these maps will help you make adjustments for next year's garden. Gardeners are always planning ahead!

When choosing a location for your garden, pay attention to your water source. Be sure to put your garden near a waterspout to which you can attach a hose. Lugging a watering can will take the fun out of gardening very quickly! It's very important to water seeds and tender young plants as soon as you put them in your garden. You will also have to water your garden when it doesn't get enough rain.

WHAT DO YOU WANT TO GROW?

Gardeners can grow native plants, hybrids, heirlooms, or some of each.

What Is a Native Plant?

A native plant has a place of origin and grows best if left in that environment. Humans have not altered native plants to meet their needs. The seeds of a native plant carry the original genetic information for its species. The saguaro cactus is native to the Sonoran Desert of the southwestern United States and northwestern Mexico. It will not grow in Pennsylvania.

Many native plants grow across a wide area. For example, the burr oak grows throughout the southern and midwestern United States. Other native species have evolved to survive only in places that meet their very special needs. Saltwort is an uncommon plant that grows only in wet, salty places where the pH is very high.

Why go native? You save time and energy. Plants grow best in the region where they evolved. Let's say you live in the town of Red Oak, in southwestern Iowa. You want to grow some flowers in your garden. You will work less—and have more time to enjoy your flowers—if you grow the locally adapted native prairie wildflowers. Some examples are purple coneflower, blazing star, and purple prairie clover.

When you grow native plants, you will attract insects and animals that rely on those plants. Bees, butterflies, hummingbirds, and bats are just a few visitors your native plants will attract. Many of these visitors, such as ladybugs and lacewings, help other plants growing in your garden by eating pests. And many of your visitors help plants reproduce by carrying pollen from flower to flower.

If you live in an arid place, planting native plants helps save water. People who live in arid places build dams and canals to bring water to the desert. Or they pump water from underground aquifers. Moving water from one place to another is very expensive. It also changes natural environments forever.

What Is a Hybrid?

When you buy seeds at a garden store or from a catalog, most likely they will be hybrid seeds.

THE Golden Rule
OF GROWING NATIVE PLANTS

Always buy or trade seeds or plants from an organization or company that deals only in nursery-raised native plant species. They should guarantee that none of their plants or seeds come from the wild. Never dig up a native plant in the wild to take home to your garden. Not only will you be upsetting a natural landscape, you may also be breaking local, state, or federal laws dealing with the protection of public lands and endangered or threatened plant species.

Plant breeders develop hybrids by breeding different plant species together. This is called crossbreeding.

The goal is to produce a plant with certain traits. A hybrid seed can contain genetic instructions that tell the plant how to fight off fungus diseases, grow faster to beat early frost, produce redder tomatoes, or make sweeter-smelling roses.

What Is an Heirloom Plant?

An heirloom is a thing of special value passed from one generation to the next. Most often we think of objects as heirlooms—your great-grandfather's pocket watch, the family china, photographs, or your mother's wedding dress. These things are priceless, because they preserve your family's history. An heirloom plant has special value, too. It preserves the history of people and places. An heirloom plant has been bred to grow in local climatic conditions. People pass these seeds from generation to generation, just as they would their other family treasures.

How does an heirloom plant differ from a native plant? A native plant is wild. The environment alone shapes the plant's genetic history. Both people and environment shape the genetic history of an heirloom. Humans select heirloom plants for special traits. They may crossbreed heirlooms to enhance those traits.

Unfortunately, heirloom plants are becoming rare.

Interested in HEIRLOOM GARDENING?

Seed Savers Exchange runs Heritage Farm near Decorah, Iowa. Here, they keep and grow an heirloom collection that includes 13,000 endangered vegetables, 700 apple varieties, 200 kinds of grapes, and a few breeds of rare livestock.

The heirloom garden at Monticello, Thomas Jefferson's estate in Virginia. Jefferson developed many different hybrids, or variations, of seeds and competed with his neighbors to bring in the earliest or largest crops.

Families and friends have stopped passing heirloom seeds down to the next generation. In the United States, scientists estimate that several thousand of our heirloom flowers, fruits, and vegetables have been lost since 1900. In the 1970s and 1980s, gardeners began to save heirloom plants. Many gardening groups, arboretums, and universities are working to see that future generations of gardeners and farmers will be able to draw from a rich bank of genetic diversity.

MAP OUT YOUR GARDEN PLAN

Already, you have spent a lot of time and brainpower picking the right place for your garden and learning about the types of plants you can grow. Now you need to make a plan. What do you want to plant? Will you be planting in a garden plot or into containers? Keep your first garden simple. Start with a few hardy plants—that is, plants that are adapted to the climate in which you garden. Gardening stores usually carry plants suited

to the local climate. If you order plants or seeds from a catalog, check the hardiness map to make sure the plant will survive in your climate. For the purposes of the activities in this book, some good choices are tomatoes, bell peppers, beans, basil, and zinnias. They are very hardy hybrid plants that will grow well in almost all parts of the United States.

Draw a Diagram

If you will be planting in a garden plot, you may want to draw a diagram of the proposed garden on graph paper. Divide the garden into separate beds for each plant. When you are ready to plant, use the drawing like a blueprint. Gardeners sometimes omit this design step and go straight to work marking off their garden beds with string. String is very helpful, because it helps you see the exact size and shape of your garden.

Most gardeners measure their garden, or they have a pretty good idea of how big it is. Let's say your garden is 10 feet (3 m) wide by 12 feet (3.7 m) long. Multiply those two numbers and you get 120 square feet (11 square meters). The

measurement will come in handy. Seeds, worms, ladybugs, and fertilizer are often sold according to the square feet they will cover.

Room to Grow

In designing your garden, read about what you are going to plant. Garden books and seed catalogs will tell you how much space to leave between plants, how big plants will grow, how much sun and water they need, and how many growing days they need to mature.

Plant in beds that are big enough to accommodate what you want to grow. Crowded plants don't get the sun and water they need to grow big and strong. And be sure to leave paths through your garden. You will need walkways to weed, water, and harvest your vegetables!

CONTAINER AND RAISED-BED GARDENING

Healthy soil is the cornerstone of gardening. But what if you don't *have* any soil? What if your soil is so sandy or silty that it is beyond rescue? What if your backyard is full of rocks? Don't worry. You can still create your own garden. Many gardeners live in high-rise apartments or in condominiums with no backyards. Some people want to grow only a few things—such as tomatoes or lettuce or a few herbs. Other gardeners do not have the time to keep a large garden. There are many ways to fit gardening into the space and time that you have.

Container Gardening

Growing flowers and vegetables in containers saves space *and* time. This method is popular in places like New York City and San Francisco, where many people do not have backyards. Container gardens are portable. When you move, you can take your garden with you. It is also a great way to try your hand at gardening. If you decide you like growing things, you can expand to a larger space.

Here are some basic rules of container gardening:

- The key to successful container gardening is giving your plants the right amount of water. To see if your plants need water, check the soil. If it is dry on the surface, poke your finger down a half-inch to an inch (1–3 cm). If the soil still feels dry, water the plant. If the soil feels moist, wait to water the plant.
- Use containers that help the soil retain moisture but also allow water to drain through the bottom. Clay pots and half barrels are excellent containers for holding moisture. But they can be heavy and expensive. Plastic pots are light and cheap. But they do not hold moisture well.

Choose a container that's big enough for the plant to grow. If you cram a plant into a small container, its roots will soon grow into a tangled mess as they try to find food and water in the soil. Make sure your containers have holes in the bottom so that water can drain out. Put your containers on trays to catch excess water.

- Place containers in bright sunshine, preferably somewhere outside.

Plants like tomatoes and green peppers need lots of sun and will not grow well inside.

- The soil you use must drain well but still retain moisture. Do not use soil taken from a garden or your backyard. Soil from outside may contain weeds, diseases, and pests. Potting soil is sterile and packed with the nutrients young plants need to grow big and strong.

Layer an inch or two (3–5 cm) of gravel or pebbles in the bottom of the container to help the plant drain properly. Make sure the gravel does not block the drainage holes. You can do this by first covering the holes with a fine mesh or with broken pieces of clay pots.

Gardening stores sell many kinds of soil mixes designed for container gardening. This soil is often called a growing medium. The best growing medium for vegetables and flowers is compost made of various ingredients, including sterilized topsoil, peat, treated manure, and sand. Make sure the growing medium you buy is fresh. If the bag looks old and dusty or the label is faded, it has probably been sitting around the garden store for a long time.

Scoop soil into the container. Then pat the soil down gently several times. Leave about 2 inches (5 cm) of space from the top of the soil to the container rim. This will keep the pot from overflowing when you water the plant. Water the growing medium to make it moist (not dripping wet). You are ready to plant.

With your hand, scoop a hole in the growing medium big enough for the root ball, or bottom, of the plant. Press the growing medium around the plant, adding more if needed. Make sure the plant is secure in its new home. You can plant several plants in a large container.

Always water after planting, even if the container is outdoors and rain is forecast. Plants grown in containers get thirsty more often than plants grown in the ground. Water is stored in tiny spaces in the soil. A large plot of ground has a much bigger reservoir of water than the soil in a container. A big garden may need water only every week or two. A plant in a container may need water every few days, especially in hot, dry weather.

Raised-Bed Gardening

Raised beds are the perfect way to garden if you have heavy, compacted soil or soil with poor drainage. Raised-bed gardening is also a very efficient use of space. Typical gardens devote lots of space to pathways. With raised beds, you walk around, not through, your garden to work. This allows you to grow twice as many vegetables or flowers in the same amount of space.

You create raised beds by tilling, or turning, the soil (by hand or with a tiller) and mixing it with a large amount of well-decomposed manure. Using a rake, you then shape the enriched soil into beds that stand several inches (centimeters) above ground level. If your soil is extremely poor, you will have to buy topsoil from a gardening store.

Making raised beds is *hard work*. It can also be expensive to purchase topsoil or composted manure or to build frames around the beds. But your investment of time, energy, and money will bring many rewards.

Size and Depth of Beds

You should design your raised beds so you can easily reach every plant. The best width is between 3 and 5 feet (90 cm and 150 cm). The length is up to you.

The soil in raised beds is usually 6 to 10 inches (15 cm to 25 cm) deep.

Frames

Putting frames around your raised beds keeps the soil from washing away. The frames also allow you to make deeper beds. You can build frames using brick, concrete blocks, rocks, or wood. If you use wood, it must resist rot. Cypress and cedar are often used as raised-bed frames. Do not use wood treated with creosote or pentachlorophenol. These are toxic substances that have no place in the garden. They will soak into the soil and, eventually, into your plants.

Raised garden beds offer opportunities to organize and show off different types of plants. They also save space and prevent erosion.

CHAPTER 2

GETTING GOING

BUYING SEEDS AND PLANTS

You can buy plants and seeds from a garden store or by mail from a catalog. The only way to find out which method you prefer is to do a little of both. Ask yourself these questions about garden stores and catalogs: Which is easier? How do their costs compare? Which teaches more about gardening? Is there a difference in the quality of the seeds and plants? And don't forget to ask yourself this: Which is more fun?

You won't get instant answers. It might take you a few years of trying both! Gardening is all about experimenting. Like many gardeners, you may end up with a favorite garden store *and* favorite catalogs. Check the phone book for garden stores in your area and ask your gardening neighbors where they shop for garden supplies.

All plants are either perennials or annuals. Purple coneflowers and chives are perennials. They pop out of the soil each spring without reseeding or planting. Tomatoes, bell peppers, beans, basil, and zinnias are annuals. Annuals live for one season and die. How do annuals keep from going extinct? Before the plant dies, it makes a fruit, vegetable, or flower that contains seeds. In the wild, these seeds scatter on the ground. They replant themselves. Or they get planted with a little help from a bird or other animal.

In the garden, you plant the seeds. How your garden grows depends on how you plant your seeds. Some gardeners start annuals from seed each year. They grow them in pots or trays in a warm place in the house and then transplant them into the garden. Other gardeners buy plants already started by a nursery. Still others sow seeds directly in the garden. Many gardeners do all three things.

STARTING SEEDS INDOORS

When you grow seeds indoors, you get a head start. Some plants need a very long time to produce the fruit, flower, or vegetable you want. Tomatoes can take eighty days. If your growing season is short, it helps to start seeds in your cozy house when it is still too cold to plant outside.

Gardeners start seeds six to eight weeks before they can plant outdoors. Don't start your seeds before this time. A plant that outgrows its pot becomes rootbound, which means its tangled, matted roots are

squeezed into too small a space. Transplanting a root-bound plant can damage it so much that it will die.

Here are some seed-planting tips: Read the instructions on your seed packets to find out how deep and how far apart to plant the seeds. Packets should also indicate how long it takes the seeds to germinate, or pop out of the ground. Many gardeners buy potting soil to start seeds. It is fluffy, it holds moisture, and it is sterile—that is, free of things that might cause diseases in tender plants.

You can buy pots and trays for starting seeds at a garden store or by mail order. Plastic pots and trays can be reused from year to year. Just wash them carefully so they are sterile. Pots made of compressed peat moss are handy because plant and pot can be planted right in your garden. The plant's roots just grow right through the pot. Or you can plant seeds in plastic yogurt or milk containers. You don't want your seeds to be waterlogged, however. Poke some holes in the bottom of the containers, so water can drain. If you have old baking pans, use them for trays for your seed pots.

TOOLS OF THE TRADE

Fortunately, there's no need to buy a lot of special tools for gardening. With a few basic tools—a shovel, spade, garden rake, hoe, pitchfork, trowel, and gloves—you could garden with great success for the rest of your life. Use a shovel for basic digging and turning of soil. For compact soils, reach for a spade, a type of shovel with a flatter blade and a pointed tip, or a pitchfork. A garden rake is handy for leveling out loosened soil and gathering up pulled weeds. When pulling up stubborn weeds, mounding up soil, creating a shallow trench for planting, or breaking up hardened soil, use a hoe. A trowel—a hand-sized shovel—is indispensable when transplanting seedlings or gardening in containers. Gloves protect your hands from slivers, glass, and sharp rocks.

Take good care of your tools, and they will serve you well for many years to come. When you are finished with a tool for the day, use a rag to wipe off any dirt or mud. Always put your tools away in a clean, dry place. Tools left out in the rain rust and wear out much earlier than tools that are properly stored. Before putting tools away for the winter, rub them with a thin layer of motor oil to prevent rust.

Set the pots in a place that is not too hot or too cold. Most seeds germinate at around 70°F (21°C), normal room temperature in most people's houses.

When the seeds sprout, make sure the plants get plenty of sunlight. Sunlight from a window will work, but be careful. Seedlings will grow toward the window. Plants are "hungry" for light and will bend over to find it. To have strong, straight plants you will have to turn your seed trays every day. Instead, put your seeds under a fluorescent light (it does not have to be a special "grow" light). Leave the light on day and night. Place the seeds about 12 inches (30 cm) from the light. Watch your seedlings carefully. If the stem of a seedling is long, thin, and pale, the plant is etiolated—it is not getting enough light.

Seeds and seedlings need to be moist. Don't flood your seeds by pouring a lot of water on them at once. A better way to water is to set your seed pots in a tray or pan and pour water into the tray. The water will soak up from the bottom. You can also use a mister to water delicate seedlings.

In late spring or early summer, when the soil outdoors has warmed up, transplant your seedlings into the garden. Before planting, you need a few days to harden your plants, which is garden talk for making them tough. It is a big shock for tender young plants to go from a greenhouse into a sunny garden. Put your plants out in the sun for an hour one day, two hours the next day, until they can stand a full day's worth of sun. Be sure to protect your plants from the wind, which can dry them out quickly and can damage the fragile leaves.

TURNING THE SOIL

Seeds and young plants like to be tucked in, just like young children do. They grow better if they are tucked in the right way. When you work the soil you are making a soft, comfortable bed for your seeds and plants. Lots of air and water can get in between the spaces in loose soil. Imagine you are a seed trying to sprout. How would you like

trying to shove your way up through hard, compact soil?

Turning your soil will be easy if you own or rent a tiller. It is a machine with sharp, curved blades that dig into the soil and flip it over. A tiller is a heavy piece of equipment that *only adults should operate*. As you can probably guess, it is also expensive. Members of community gardens often pool their money to buy a tiller. It is not something you want to buy if your garden is small. Here's how to prepare the soil.

Shovel! It is best to turn the soil right before planting. If you do it days or weeks in advance, you are wasting your energy. The soil will just crust over and compact again. Start with one of the beds you are ready to plant. Dig up a shovelful of soil and turn it over. Go as deep as the shovel blade. (Many gardeners "double-dig," which means they dig to a depth equal to two shovel blades. That's *really* hard work!) If you have

a pitchfork, you may want to use that instead. It crumbles and breaks up the soil as you turn it.

Crumble! After you dig up a row—or when you need to rest!—put down the shovel and start working the soil in your hands. You may wish to use gloves at this point, especially if you are working in an area where there is broken glass and metal scraps. Break up the big clods of dirt. Crumble the soil until the particles are all about the size of golf balls. If you are digging through grass to create your garden plot, separate the grass from the dirt at this point.

Rake! Take a garden rake (not a leaf rake) and smooth the soil. Make the bed as level as possible, so water won't run off too fast or puddle in low spots.

IMPROVING YOUR SOIL WITH COMPOST

Many gardeners make compost from leaves, grass clippings, and kitchen scraps. Gardeners call compost "black gold." It improves soil that is too sandy and soil with too much clay. It helps soil hold water and gives soil more space to hold air. Compost is also full of nutrients. Gardeners add compost when they turn the soil. As they dig, they toss in a handful of compost to fill each hole about halfway, and then they use the shovel or rake to work it into the soil. If you do not have the room or the energy to make your own compost, buy some at your local garden store.

By composting, you are giving back to the earth what you have taken from it. The organic matter you put in your compost provides a gourmet meal for millions of earthworms, beetles, snails, bacteria, fungi, molds, and protozoans. These hungry decomposers convert all the living stuff that dies into reusable products. In turn, they will nourish your garden.

Some gardeners turn composting into hard work. Others keep it simple. The simplest compost is a pile of organic matter. The pile has one big problem: it is easy for dogs, cats, raccoons, and other critters in your neighborhood to raid it. For that reason, it is better to compost in a bin or similar enclosure that keeps out unwanted visitors. Surround your compost with four stakes and enclose the pile with chicken wire. An ideal size and shape for a backyard compost bin is 3 feet by 3 feet by 3 feet (90 cm by 90 cm by 90 cm), or a cubic yard. If your compost bin is too small, the heat drifts away, and the organic matter never heats up—or takes forever to heat up. If the bin is too big, the stuff will cook in the middle but not on the outside.

Feeding Your Compost
Just like you, the decomposers in your compost need a balanced diet. Carbon is the basic building block of all living things. Each living organism has its own special arrangement of carbon.

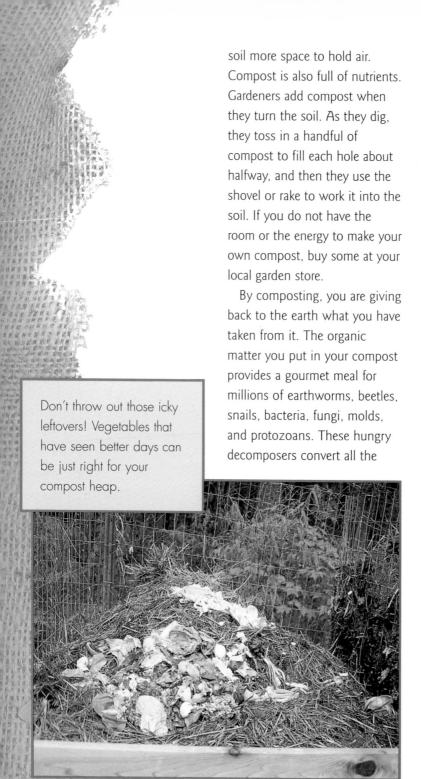

Don't throw out those icky leftovers! Vegetables that have seen better days can be just right for your compost heap.

Hot Stuff:

The Science of Composting

As organic matter decays, energy is released in the form of heat. This is why compost heats up or "cooks." The billions of decomposers in your compost work at different temperatures. One group of decomposing microorganisms, called psychrophiles, work when the temperature in the compost is cool, 55°F (13°C) or less. They are busy in your compost even on a cold day. As they chomp away, the compost heats up. The mesophile microorganisms then go into action. They are most efficient when temperatures linger between 70° and 90°F (21–32°C). When the heat rises higher, the thermophile microorganisms step up to the salad bar. These decomposers like a really hot environment—between 112° and 150°F (44–66°C).

Your goal is to get your compost's temperature hot enough to get those thermophiles to work. By the time it reaches about 140°F (60°C), your organic matter has been picked over by many munchers. It is well decayed. At these high temperatures, germs and weed seeds will be killed.

It's important to take your compost's temperature, around once a week. For super-accurate readings, you can buy a compost thermometer. But most gardeners use a three-foot-long (1m-long) metal rod. They stick it in the middle of the compost for five to ten minutes, take it out, and feel it. This method is similar to your mother or father touching your forehead to see if you have a fever. And it works just as well. This is how gardeners "read" the rod:

Cool. If the rod feels cooler than your own body, the decay process is moving very slowly. Some gardeners prefer this slow, cool composting method. Others want to boost the temperature, so they add more organic stuff.

Warmish to hot. The compost's temperature is in the 130° to 140°F (54–60°C) zone. Decay is going along smoothly.

Really hot. The thermophiles are too busy. It is time to turn the stuff over and release some of the heat.

It's easy to feed carbon to your compost, because all organic matter is composed of it.

Your compost also needs nitrogen, but in much smaller amounts. Nitrogen helps form proteins that perform many important tasks in all living things, from fungi to you. For example, many proteins jump-start important biochemical reactions that occur within cells. Good sources of nitrogen include grass clippings, coffee grounds, and the manure of horses, cows, and chickens. But your compost can have too much nitrogen. When that happens, you will know it—the pile will stink. The excess nitrogen escapes as ammonia gas. Add straw, dry leaves, and shredded paper and newsprint, all of which are rich in carbon. The smell will go away quickly.

The perfect carbon-nitrogen diet for your decomposers is about 30 parts carbon to 1 part nitrogen. Fortunately, you do not have to be an organic chemist to keep your fungi, bacteria, and other decomposers happy and well fed. Most gardeners feed their compost a mixture of dry leaves, grass clippings, peelings from fruits and vegetables, old lettuce, leftover vegetables, eggshells, tea bags, coffee grounds, and manure and let the decomposers go to work. Other good stuff for the compost in limited amounts includes lint from your clothes dryer, cardboard, newspapers (if the ink is soy-based), straw, hay, sawdust, dog and cat hair, wool, and seaweed (if you wash away the coating of salt).

Manure is a great addition to compost. It is an excellent source of nitrogen, and it already contains a swarm of bacteria, fungi, and other hungry decomposers. By adding manure, you will speed up the decaying process in your compost.

Decomposers need water and oxygen, too. Keep your compost moist, but not soggy, by spraying it lightly with a hose. Let it breathe by turning over the organic material. Sooner or later, the end result will be crumbly, earthy-smelling soil to put on your garden.

What Not to Put in Your Compost
There are many things you should not put in your compost. Do not compost the poop of your pet dog, cat, or bird. Their manure can contain germs harmful to humans. Your compost may not make

enough heat to kill the pathogens (disease-causing agents). Although meat and dairy products are organic matter, they attract animals and can smell awful while decomposing. Be thoughtful of your neighbors and don't add meat or dairy to your compost.

Citrus is another example of organic matter not suited for composting. The thick skins of oranges, grapefruits, lemons, and limes take forever to decay. If you try to compost citrus, it may still be in your backyard compost slowly withering away years from now.

The leaves of magnolias, holly, and some oaks are like shoe leather. You probably wouldn't put old shoes in your compost. Don't put in these kinds of leaves either. Some plants contain natural toxins, or poisons. These poisons protect a plant from predators or they kill its competition. Walnut, eucalyptus, and oleander are three plants with toxic leaves. Do not put their leaves in your compost. Find out the names of the trees and shrubs growing in your yard and be sure they do not contain toxic substances.

Do not compost weeds that have sprouted seed heads. If you do, those weeds may come back to haunt you. If your compost does not heat up enough to kill the seeds, you will have a whole new crop of weeds when you spread the compost on your garden.

Don't compost grass clippings from chemically treated lawns. Grass clippings are great compost food—unless they come from lawns sprayed with weed killer and fertilizer.

There is a simple way to tell when your compost is ready: scoop up a handful and crumble it. Your eyes, fingers, and nose will tell you if the decomposition process is done. If it looks, feels, and smells like rich, crumbly, black soil, your compost is ready.

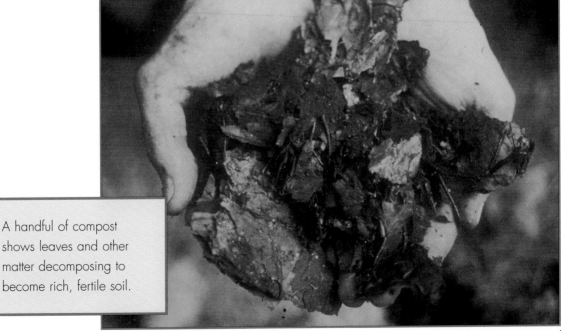

A handful of compost shows leaves and other matter decomposing to become rich, fertile soil.

CHAPTER 3

INTO THE GROUND

Planting day has arrived! You have turned the soil in your beds. Resist the temptation to plant everything at once. For vegetable gardens, it is better to plant a little at a time. For example, if you put in a few rows of green beans every two weeks, you will have just the right amount of beans to eat. By planting several small crops, you will not have the problem of too much produce to eat! Of course, you can always give extra vegetables to friends. Homegrown food is a great gift.

Some plants, such as peas and spinach, actually do better when planted in cooler temperatures early in the spring. Tomatoes and peppers, on the other hand, thrive in hot weather and will not do well if planted at the same time as peas. Read the instructions on your seed packets or plants. They will tell you the best time to put the seeds or plants into the ground.

SEEDS OR PLANTS?

Some plants need a head start, especially in zones where the growing season is short. Tomatoes take seventy to eighty days to produce fruit. Bell peppers take a long time, too. Zinnias bloom in about sixty days. These are examples of plants that you will want to buy or start from seed.

Beans take fifty to sixty-five days. You can pick basil leaves in forty days or less. Most gardeners plant these seeds directly in the garden. Other easy plants to start from seed are sunflowers, cosmos, marigolds, lettuces, radishes, and peas. Read books, catalogs, and seed packets. Ask other gardeners and experiment. You will soon know the answer to the question, "Seeds or plants?"

SOWING SEEDS

When gardeners take seeds right from the packet and pop them into the ground, it is called direct seeding. Plants that are hardy and grow quickly do very well by this method. It's simple. But you have to be patient. If you direct seed too early in the spring, when the soil is still cold, the seeds will never sprout.

Check the soil in your beds once again just before planting your seeds. The soil should be loose and soft—almost fluffy. Use a rake or your hands to break up any clods that may have formed. The easiest way to start planting is to use your finger or the edge of a hoe or trowel to create a trench.

SEEDS of LIFE

Seeds are like little suitcases. They are packed with all the stuff a plant needs to sprout, grow, and reproduce. It's amazing to think that a redwood, the largest tree in the world, grows from a seed smaller than your little fingernail.

Conditions have to be right for the "suitcase" to open. The outside layer of the seed—called the seed coat—is designed to open when it receives the right amount of water, sunlight, and warmth.

The seed coats of many desert plants burst open only after enough rain falls. A special chemical in the seed coat has to be washed away before the seed will germinate. A brief rain can't do the job. When the chemical is gone, the seed gets a message that there is enough water for it to sprout and grow.

Sunlight also plays a part in opening the seed suitcase. Some kinds of lettuce will not germinate without light. Poppy and geranium seeds, on the other hand, germinate only in the dark!

Read the seed packet to see how deep and how far apart to plant the seeds. Then drop seeds in the trench. Carefully cover the seeds with soil and pat it down. Gently soak the planted seeds with water.

WATERING TIPS

Water seeds right after you plant them, using a gentle spray. You don't want to wash your seeds away. Keep the beds moist until the seeds germinate. If a hard, dry crust forms on the soil, it will be hard for the seeds to poke through.

After the first few weeks, your garden will do better if you water it less. Once a garden gets going, it may need to be watered only once or twice a season, depending on how regularly it rains. Water only when your garden really needs it.

Keep in mind that some plants need more water than others. Purple coneflowers, for example, grow best when the soil is on the dry side. Tomatoes, on the other hand, need lots more water to produce big, juicy fruit.

Use a soaker hose, instead of a sprinkler. A soaker hose has many tiny holes poked in it. Water oozes from the hose and sinks directly into the ground and to the roots. A sprinkler throws water into the air, where some of it evaporates and never gets to your garden.

MULCH

Placing mulch, or a protective covering of grass clippings, around your plants keeps water from evaporating from the soil. Some gardeners use black plastic, but it costs money. Grass clippings are free. Keep grass clippings from touching the stems of the plants, because the nitrogen in them can burn the stems.

BUYING PLANTS

There are good reasons for *not* starting seeds indoors. It takes time and space, and tender seedlings need lots of attention. Some plants are very hard to grow from seed. They need expert care and special conditions to sprout.

If you decide to buy your plants, don't wait until the last minute. You will not have much

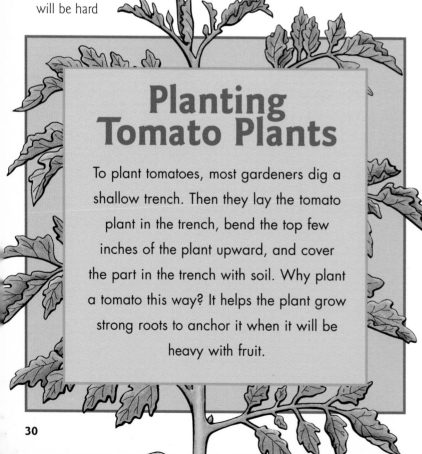

Planting Tomato Plants

To plant tomatoes, most gardeners dig a shallow trench. Then they lay the tomato plant in the trench, bend the top few inches of the plant upward, and cover the part in the trench with soil. Why plant a tomato this way? It helps the plant grow strong roots to anchor it when it will be heavy with fruit.

variety to pick from, because other gardeners will have beat you to it!

Before you buy or start your own tomato plants, you will need to think about which kind you want to grow. There are two basic types of tomatoes. Determinate tomatoes are bushy, compact plants that produce tomatoes that all ripen in a fairly short time. That means your harvest time will also be short—and busy. Beefsteak and Early Girl are both determinate varieties. Indeterminate tomatoes, such as yellow pear tomatoes and cherry tomatoes, continue to make fruits over a longer period of time. As a rule, indeterminate varieties grow bigger than determinate varieties and require cages or stakes to hold them upright.

TRANSPLANTING SEEDLINGS

When transplanting seedlings, always be quick, but gentle. Use a trowel (or your hand) to dig a hole in the soil for the seedling. Think of the hole as clothes—a dress or a pair of pants. You want the hole to fit the plant. As a rule, the hole should be just a bit bigger than the plant's ball of roots.

If your seedling is in a pot made of peat moss, plant the whole thing in the ground. The roots will simply grow through the peat. If your seedling is in a plastic pot, place your fingers and palm over the top of the pot, careful not to crush the seedling, and turn the pot upside down. Gently squeeze the sides of the pot. The plant, roots and all, should fall out into your hand. Turn the plant right side up and put it in the hole you have prepared. Gently push soil into and around the roots. Pat the soil down. Water your transplants right away. *Never omit this step.* Water helps the soil settle around the roots.

It is a good habit to inspect your garden at least once a day. Keep an eye on your new transplants. Make sure the soil stays moist. Spread mulch as needed.

At first your transplants may not grow at all. That's because they are getting over the shock of being moved to a new home. In a week or two, their roots will take hold and start pumping in food, water, and minerals to make the plants grow.

GETTING A GRIP

Roots are as important to a plant as your arms and legs are to you. Roots anchor a plant in wind, snow, ice, rain, and floods. They help a plant stand up when it is loaded with heavy vegetables. And roots have an amazing ability to find water and nutrients in the soil and then transport these to the rest of the plant.

When transplanting, think about roots. They are designed for life underground. They like to be hugged by soil. They do not like to be disturbed, so transplanting is a big shock for them. Unless you are careful, the roots may be so damaged that they never recover. Your seedling, which you have already spent time and effort to grow, will die. Handle transplants with care.

CHAPTER 4

HOW DOES YOUR GARDEN GROW?

From planting until harvesttime, you have one job—to keep an eye on your garden. Try to visit your garden every day, or even better, twice a day. Get to know your plants. The more you look, the more you'll learn.

GO ON PATROL!

Gardeners love to patrol their gardens. Every day in your garden is different, and every year unlike the year before. Even people who garden for a long time find new things.

Garden patrols, of course, have an important purpose. Be on the lookout for weeds, insect pests, and disease. Some gardeners take a grim view of these things. For them, it is a battle against the enemy. But remember the wise words of the English gardener Hugh Johnson: "Everything that grows is food for something else." Weeds, insects, and the pathogens that cause disease are simply competing with you. You will never get rid of the competition, but you can control it.

WHAT IS A WEED?

A weed is any plant you do not want growing in your garden. Weeds take up space, soak up sunlight, and suck nutrients and water from the soil. The more of these resources the weeds take, the less there will be to nourish your flowers and vegetables.

On your garden patrols, pull weeds up by hand or scrape them up at ground level with the straight edge of a hoe. Another way to control weeds is to smother them with mulch. Mulch keeps weeds in the dark. Without sunlight, weeds will die. Some sunlight will filter through grass clippings, so a few weeds will survive. But weeds that manage to poke through mulch are weak from lack of sun. They are easy (and fun) to pull.

Some gardeners use black plastic mulch. It *really* keeps out the sun. But it is an extra expense. And, at the end of the year, it is trash. Grass clippings don't cost anything and will improve your soil as they decompose.

Should you use a weed killer? In a small garden, it is easy to control weeds by hand and with mulch. Weeding is also a good way for you to get to know the competition. Chemicals that kill weeds can be useful in large gardens. However, chemicals are expensive, and they can be dangerous. Never use a weed killer without the help of an adult gardener.

INSECTS, GOOD AND BAD

Most insects, you will find, go about their business, doing little or no harm to your garden. Organic gardeners live happily with insects. They encourage beneficial insects and find safe, nontoxic ways to get rid of the pesky ones. Beneficial insects pollinate flowers. They burrow in the soil, making space for oxygen. And, best of all, some of them eat the competition!

Ladybugs, for example, eat aphids, scale insects, and mites. For that reason, many gardeners let ladybugs loose in the garden to control pests. You can buy ladybugs through most gardening stores.

They are usually sold by the half-pint or pint and are shipped in the mail directly to your house. It's also a good idea to leave caterpillars alone, especially if you're growing plants to attract butterflies to your garden. Since butterflies start out as caterpillars, treat them as friends rather than foes.

Some of the competition for our favorite vegetables are tiny insects. These green peach aphids are feeding on a cabbage leaf.

Learning about the Competition

Looking for insect pests is like being Sherlock Holmes in the garden. Many of the insects are too tiny to see, or they work only at night. You have to watch for clues. Here are three of the most common garden pests and ways to outsmart them.

- Aphids are not much bigger than the head of a pin. The green insects like to cluster on stems and branches, so they are easy to spot. Aphids suck the juices out of your plants and transmit viruses that make your plants sick. To get rid of them, spray water on the aphid-covered stems. The force of the water will knock the pests off the plant. If the aphids return, order some ladybugs or other aphid-eating insects and release them in your garden as soon as possible. Soap is another anti-aphid product. Mix 4 teaspoons (20 ml) of mild dish detergent with a quart (0.9 l) of water. Put the mixture in a spray bottle and mist the aphids. The soap makes stems slippery and the aphids can't get a grip. Look for soap made just for this purpose at a garden supply store. This soap will not hurt the plants.

The colorful but deadly Colorado potato beetle munches on the foliage of a potato plant.

•Cutworms are not worms at all but the larvae of noctuid moths. Cutworms can mow through a garden, feeding on roots and shoots of young plants. You seldom see cutworms, but they leave obvious clues. They chomp stems off right at ground level.

Prevent cutworm damage by protecting your young stems. Remove the ends of tin cans or plastic containers and gently push these into the ground around young plants. Many gardeners make a habit of putting these "fences" around all their newly planted seedlings. The guards also protect young plants from heavy rains and prevent pets from tromping on them.

•Colorado potato beetles are found in gardens across North America. The beetles eat the leaves of potatoes, tomatoes, eggplants, and peppers. The adults are yellow with black stripes on their bodies and black dots on their heads. The larvae are red with black heads and legs. In the spring, they move into gardens to feed and lay their eggs. To defeat them, put a thick layer of mulch around young plants. Adult Colorado potato beetles have trouble finding plants hidden in mulch. Ladybugs and spined soldier bugs are two beneficial insects that feed on the larvae of Colorado potato beetles. Set some loose in the garden and let them feast.

Who's on Your Team?

You may be surprised at the insects that are good for your garden. For example, hornets and their cousins, yellow jackets, gobble up lots of flies and insect larvae. Many gardeners are happy to share their gardens with hungry hornets and yellow jackets. At the same time, they respect possible hazards. Some people have severe allergic reactions to wasp stings. In this case, hornet and yellow jacket nests should be removed. Leave this job to an adult with experience in handling wasp nests.

Here is a list of beneficial insects and other critters that are on your team.

- **Ladybugs are little Volkswagen-shaped beetles.** They are usually bright red with black spots, but some are orange or yellow. Most garden stores can tell you how to order a bag of ladybugs to release in your garden.
- Adult lacewings are dainty insects with shimmering wings that look almost like cellophane. **The most common lacewings are lime-green.**

A ladybug makes a meal of a bunch of aphids. Ladybugs are colorful beetles that can be very helpful in attacking the pests in your garden.

If you pick one up, be careful. When disturbed, the adults can emit a stinky odor. It is the larvae of lacewings that are useful to gardeners. One little lacewing larva can eat hundreds of aphids. No wonder lacewing larvae are called aphid lions. Lacewings are sold in garden stores as eggs. Scatter the tiny eggs around in your garden. When they hatch, the larvae go to work eating aphids.

•Dragonflies and damselflies are helicopter-like insects that really know how to fly. They fly up, down, and backward, eating midges, mosquitoes, and gnats along the way.

•Nematodes are worms, not insects. They are one of the most abundant forms of life on the earth, but you never see them. These tiny worms live in the soil or in water. Beneficial nematodes attack and eat garden pests that live underground, such as cutworms and white grubs. Because nematodes emit a toxin to paralyze and kill their prey, they are able to kill things that are far bigger than they are. You can buy nematodes to put in your garden. Even a small package contains millions of them. You mix the nematodes with water and pour them onto your garden. They are very sensitive to sunlight and air. Follow instructions carefully, so your investment in nematodes does not "go down the drain."

MAKE YOUR GARDEN TOAD-FRIENDLY

A toad or two in your garden is a priceless gift. These pest-o-vacs eat just about every unwanted garden invader, including slugs, grubs, cutworms, and grasshoppers. To attract toads to your garden, grow some plants in your yard that are native to your area. It will make a toad feel at home. A yard that is mostly lawn will seem like Mars to a toad. Don't use pesticides and fertilizers in your yard. Don't rake all the leaves under trees and shrubs. Make a burrow where a toad can hide and get some shade. A shallow hole with a board over it will work.

Put up a toad light. Place it near the border of your garden on a post about 3 feet (1 m) high. The light will attract insects; the insects will attract a toad. With a nightlight, a toad will eat about 3,200 insects in a season.

Smart gardeners love to see a garter snake or ribbon snake slithering between their plants. Snakes eat insects, slugs, and snails. Most snakes in North America are harmless and very shy. They depart quickly when they detect people nearby. The four species of poisonous snakes found in North America are rarely found in towns and cities, where most people have gardens. If you are concerned about snakes, contact your county extension service to make sure none of the snakes in your region are poisonous.

ATTRACT BENEFICIAL INSECTS

Make your garden a welcome place for pollinating insects. Flowering plants produce pollen grains. These are packets of genetic information that plants must share to reproduce. Getting pollen grains from one flower to the next is called pollination. Plants must be pollinated to produce vegetables and fruit. Wind and water can carry pollen. But in your garden, insects are the most important pollen delivery service. As they

feed on a flower's nectar, insects get covered in tiny pollen grains. When they fly to the next flower, they leave behind some pollen. Bees do most of the pollination work in your garden. But various butterflies, moths, and wasps also pollinate plants. Without pollination, all the hard work you put into gardening will be wasted.

To attract pollinators to your garden, plant flowers in and around your vegetable garden. Some of the best plants for attracting pollinators are buckwheat, dill, morning glory, zinnias, sunflowers, yarrow, and clover. Besides providing food and shelter for insects, these plantings make your garden more colorful.

Draw other beneficial insects to your garden with the promise of shelter. Mulch and scattered leaves provide beneficial insects with "umbrellas" from the heat and sun. These same shady places can also provide shade for insect pests. This is one of the lessons of gardening. You have to take the bad with the good.

Water attracts insects, too. When it rains, or when you water your garden, insects can drink droplets on leaves or from puddles. Garden writer Jeff Cox suggests placing a shallow birdbath or bowl in your garden and filling it with rocks and water. The rocks will provide landing pads for beneficial insects so they can drink without drowning. Every so often, rinse out the birdbath and fill it with clean water.

FIGHT DISEASE

Bacteria, viruses, and fungi make plants sick, just as they infect people. Disease-causing agents are called pathogens. It takes years of gardening experience to learn about all the plant diseases and symptoms. There are blights, mildews, molds, rusts, and wilts, just to mention a few. It is easier to *prevent* a disease than to *cure* it. Take care of your garden's health the same way you take care of yourself.

Grow plants that are disease resistant. Many seed companies develop seeds that resist diseases. Read carefully in seed catalogs or ask clerks in garden stores to find out if you are buying seeds and plants that can fight off pathogens. For example, many varieties of tomatoes are resistant to the common tomato diseases fusarium wilt, verticillium wilt, and tobacco mosaic virus.

Keep your garden clean. Piles of brush or other vegetation are breeding grounds for pathogens. Don't make places for diseases to grow and spread.

Guard against molds and mildews. Molds and mildews are caused by fungi, and fungi love damp, dark places. Don't crowd your plants. Make sure enough light and air can get to each plant.

Call for help! When you are on patrol, look carefully at the leaves of your plants. Many plant diseases cause spots, blotches, or wilting. If your plants look really sick or if they are dying, call your county extension office and describe the symptoms. Your county agent will be able to give you advice on what to do.

SUPPORT YOUR PLANTS

Vines and plants that produce heavy fruits need your help. Beans, peppers, and tomatoes are common garden plants that require support. You can use stakes, trellises, or cages to help support them. Gardeners usually use cages for tomatoes, trellises for beans, and stakes for peppers. When you provide support for plants, it makes it easier for you to weed around them and to harvest from them. The support also helps keep fruits and vegetables from lying on the soil, where they will rot quickly.

You can buy stakes, cages, and trellises at garden shops, or you can invent your own, using materials you find in your garage or basement. Old broom handles make good stakes. You can use chicken wire to make a tomato cage. Make a trellis for beans by rigging heavy twine on a wooden fence or wall. Train the bean vines to grow up the string by guiding them as they grow.

A stake must be tall and strong enough to support a full-grown plant during rains and high winds. Sink the stake into the ground close to the stem of the plant when it is 6 to 8 inches (15 to 20 cm) tall. As the plant grows, use string, strips of cloth, or old pantyhose to tie the stem loosely to the stake.

CHAPTER 5
HARVEST

Harvesttime is your reward for months of hard work. Garden catalogs often tell how many days from the time of planting it will take for each vegetable variety to mature. The same information is also printed on seed packets. Use this information as a general guide to when you should harvest, but remember that factors like climate and rainfall will affect how your plants mature.

It is best to harvest your vegetables in the middle of the morning. The dew has dried off the plants, but the day is still cool. Take a walk through your garden and look at all the ways you can gather, store, prepare, and share your produce.

TOMATOES

Tomatoes are the most common plants in American gardens. Gardeners know that a vine-ripened tomato tastes better than a tomato trucked cross-country to the grocery store. Tomatoes need hot sun to make the sugars that give them their special acidic sweet taste. Most store tomatoes are harvested green and never get that final dose of hot sun. Tomatoes are loaded with vitamins A and C. The amount of these vitamins increases as the fruit ripens on the vine.

Harvest tomatoes after they turn red on the vine. To test for ripeness, gently squeeze the red tomato. If it is hard, it is not quite ripe. If it gives a little, it is ready to pick. Cut the fruit off the vine with scissors. Grabbing and pulling can break branches and knock unripe

TIME

tomatoes off the vine. If you planted a determinate variety, your tomatoes will ripen all at once. If you planted an indeterminate variety, the plants will make fruits over a longer period of time.

If you planted too many tomatoes and are afraid that an early frost will zap your garden before you can harvest all of them, pull up the tomato plants and hang them upside down by their roots in your garage or basement. In the next four to six weeks, the fruits will slowly ripen on the dying vines.

Tomatoes offer so many possibilities, you may have trouble deciding what to do with them. Even people who have gardened for many years still find new ways to prepare and preserve tomatoes.

Tomatoes can be eaten straight off the vine in salads and salsas and on sandwiches. You can cook them, freeze them, dry them, or can them. Canning, which really means storing your tomatoes in jars, must be done *very* carefully. You must avoid contaminating the contents with bacteria that could make you sick. If you want to can your tomatoes, it's important to work with a person who has experience in preserving fruits and vegetables. You will find many books in the library full of information on how to use and store tomatoes.

BELL PEPPERS

Peppers grow slowly and take a long time to mature. They will be one of the last things you harvest in your garden. Bell peppers, also called sweet peppers, are a very important ingredient for cooks around the world.

FOOD BANKS

Although some people have plenty of food to eat, many others do not. Sharing is one way to help balance the unequal access to food. But sharing in today's complex world can be hard. Sharing involves moving food from a place of plenty to a place of need. In the late 1960s, a retired businessman named John Van Hengel started to volunteer at a soup kitchen in Phoenix, Arizona. He knew that a lot of food went to waste in parts of his community, so he began to ask businesses to donate this extra food, instead of throwing it away. Soon the soup kitchen had more food than it could use. So Mr. Van Hengel started a warehouse to store and distribute food to people in need all over the city. This was the beginning of the modern food bank.

The food bank idea spread around the country. In 1979 America's Second Harvest was founded. It helped people set up food bank warehouses, and it became a national clearinghouse for large food donations from major corporations. By 2000, America's Second Harvest had grown to be the largest charitable hunger-relief organization in the United States. It has a network of more than two thousand food banks and food-rescue programs in the United States and Puerto Rico. Each year, it provides food assistance to about twenty-six million people.

Bell peppers cooked along with onions and celery are the basis of many Cajun dishes, like gumbo, jambalaya, and étouffée. Peppers provide vitamins A and C.

You can harvest bell peppers when they are green. If you have a long growing season, leave the peppers on the vine. They will continue to ripen and, depending on the variety, turn beautiful shades of red, purple, or yellow. The longer the peppers ripen, the more flavor and nutrition they will have.

You can eat sweet peppers uncooked as a snack or in salads. You can stuff them with meat or rice and bake them. You can roast them on the grill, stir-fry them, and put them in soups. Bell peppers are best eaten fresh from the garden. You can also freeze them to use later in soups and other cooking. Wash and dry them, remove the stems and seeds, leave whole or cut into pieces, put in plastic bags and freeze.

BEANS

Beans are good for you and for your garden. They are a source of vitamins A and C, calcium, and iron. And they improve

These mature green beans are ready for harvesting. By picking some beans every day, gardeners encourage the vine to continue to grow more beans throughout the harvest season.

your soil. Rhizobium bacteria in the soil form nodules, or bumps, on bean roots. These nodules take nitrogen from the air and convert it to ammonia, which helps all plants grow big and strong. This process is called nitrogen fixation. Rhizobium bacteria can make almost ten times more nitrogen than the bacteria need. The extra ammonia helps your beans grow and enriches your garden soil. Next year, plant tomatoes in that fortified soil. Move your bean crop to another part of the garden to enrich the soil there.

Pick beans when they are young and tender. And pick them every few days. As long as you continue to pick beans, the plant will continue to make

them. If you wait until your beans are old, they will be tough and stringy, and you won't have as many beans to eat. Harvesting beans is like hunting for Easter eggs. You have to look hard and long! The beans may be hiding under vines and leaves. Just when you think you have picked the last one, you will see another. It helps to harvest beans with a friend. Four eyes are better than two eyes when looking for hidden beans.

Buried in beans? Eating beans for breakfast, lunch, and dinner?

Beans can be dried, canned, or pickled. But most gardeners will tell you that beans are best fresh from the garden. The best thing to do with your bean surplus is share it with friends and neighbors. If you live in a large city, call the local food bank to see if they accept garden vegetables. Try selling your produce. Set up a vegetable stand and test the market in your neighborhood. And next year, plant fewer beans.

SWEET BASIL

Sweet basil belongs to the mint family, a group of plants including peppermint and spearmint that are known for producing strongly scented oils. Humans use the oils to make things like chewing gum. The oils help protect the plant from insects, which don't like the strong smell. Sweet basil, an important herb in Italian and Asian cooking, is very fragrant and flavorful. Gardeners often plant basil just because it makes the garden smell so good.

Basil and other plants used for flavor, aroma, dye, or medicine are called herbs. The edible part of the basil plant is the leaves. As soon as your basil has lots of leaves, you can start picking or cutting them. You can harvest basil all summer and into the fall. As soon as your basil plants start to flower, pinch off those flower heads when you are on your garden patrols. This will encourage the plant to direct its energy into making leaves.

Fresh basil adds zing to your food. Throw basil leaves in a salad, drop a sprig in your soup, or put basil on your sandwich. Many gardeners grow basil so they can make pesto and freeze it. That way, they can enjoy the fresh, summery taste of basil all winter long. Use pesto as a sauce on spaghetti, as a sandwich spread, or to flavor soup.

ZINNIAS

Zinnias come in a wide range of colors and sizes. Dwarf zinnias grow low to the ground in tight mounds only 6 to 12 inches (15 to 30 cm) tall. Classic zinnias grow about 10 inches (25 cm) tall. Taller varieties can reach 3 feet (90 cm), with blooms as big as 7 inches (20 cm) across.

Cut zinnias for flower arrangements just after the blooms have opened. Use scissors to cut the stem at the length appropriate to the vase or container in which you will be arranging the flowers.

After cutting from the plant, trim the stems at an angle. This allows the flowers to "drink" water with ease. Remove any leaves from the cut flowers that look as if they will fall beneath the waterline of the vase. If left on the plant, these leaves rot and make the water smell.

Immediately transfer cut flowers to cold water. Arrange the flowers as desired and place the vase in a spot where the flowers can be enjoyed. To keep them fresh, remove them from the vase and retrim the stems daily. Pour out the old water and replace it with fresh, cold water.

RECIPES FOR GARDENERS

Many gardeners also love to cook. Here are some easy recipes for your harvest. With the help of an adult, you can prepare some wonderful things to eat.

Salsa

Salsas are sauces used in Latin American cooking. Salsa can be eaten as a dip with corn chips, or you can use it as you would ketchup—on meat or in a sandwich. Try putting a spoonful in a bowl of stew or soup or on your mashed potatoes! Here is a recipe for tomato salsa from *Authentic Mexican*, a cookbook by Rick and Deann Bayless. They are experts on the foods of Mexico and have a restaurant in Chicago, Illinois.

- **1 large ripe tomato, cored and chopped**
- **1 green serrano or jalapeño pepper (this will make the salsa very hot, so use a bell pepper if you don't like spicy food)**
- **1 small onion, finely chopped**
- **1 clove of garlic, peeled and chopped**
- **8 to 10 sprigs of cilantro, chopped**
- **1 tablespoon (15 ml) water**
- **½ teaspoon salt**
- **1 teaspoon (5 ml) lime juice (or cider vinegar)**

If you use the hot chile, wear rubber gloves to protect your hands. Remove the core and seeds from the chile pepper and chop it into small pieces. Put all the ingredients in a bowl and stir to combine. Allow the flavors of the salsa to mingle for 30 minutes before tasting.

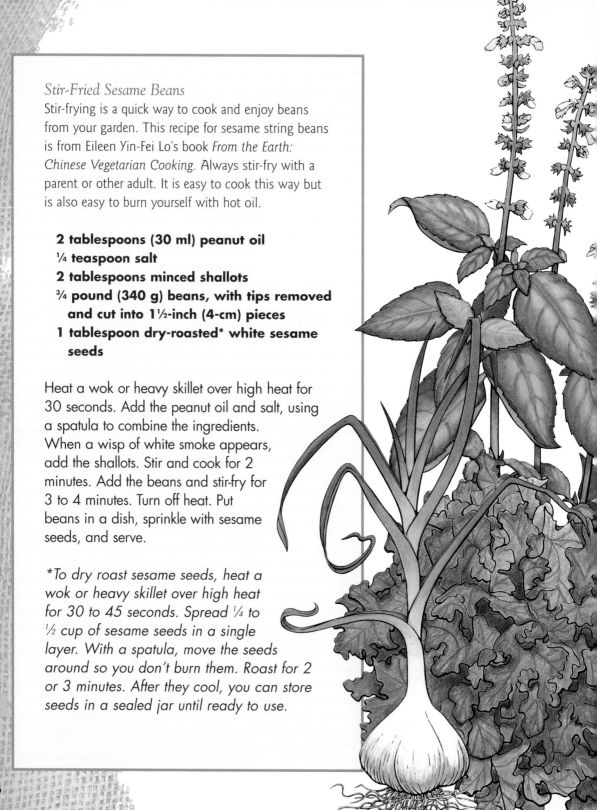

Stir-Fried Sesame Beans

Stir-frying is a quick way to cook and enjoy beans from your garden. This recipe for sesame string beans is from Eileen Yin-Fei Lo's book *From the Earth: Chinese Vegetarian Cooking.* Always stir-fry with a parent or other adult. It is easy to cook this way but is also easy to burn yourself with hot oil.

- **2 tablespoons (30 ml) peanut oil**
- **¼ teaspoon salt**
- **2 tablespoons minced shallots**
- **¾ pound (340 g) beans, with tips removed and cut into 1½-inch (4-cm) pieces**
- **1 tablespoon dry-roasted* white sesame seeds**

Heat a wok or heavy skillet over high heat for 30 seconds. Add the peanut oil and salt, using a spatula to combine the ingredients. When a wisp of white smoke appears, add the shallots. Stir and cook for 2 minutes. Add the beans and stir-fry for 3 to 4 minutes. Turn off heat. Put beans in a dish, sprinkle with sesame seeds, and serve.

*To dry roast sesame seeds, heat a wok or heavy skillet over high heat for 30 to 45 seconds. Spread ¼ to ½ cup of sesame seeds in a single layer. With a spatula, move the seeds around so you don't burn them. Roast for 2 or 3 minutes. After they cool, you can store seeds in a sealed jar until ready to use.

Sweet Basil Pesto

Marcella Hazan is famous for her Italian cookbooks. Here is her recipe for basil pesto, which freezes very well. This recipe requires a blender, so do not make it without help from a parent or other grown-up.

2 cups fresh basil leaves
½ cup (120 ml) olive oil
2 tablespoons pine nuts
2 garlic cloves, peeled and crushed
1 teaspoon salt
½ cup grated Parmesan cheese
2 tablespoons grated Romano cheese (optional)

Combine the basil leaves, olive oil, pine nuts, garlic, and salt in a blender and mix at high speed. Stop the blender and use a rubber spatula to push the pesto toward the bottom of the blender. Continue to blend until you have a green soupy mixture. Spoon the mixture into small yogurt cups or into ice-cube trays and put in freezer. When frozen, pop out cubes and transfer them to a plastic freezer bag. Freeze until ready to use. Take pesto from the freezer and let it defrost. When it is soft, stir in the cheese. Store the pesto in jars in the refrigerator. The sauce will keep for a week or so.

Stuffed Bell Peppers

Fresh, crisp bell peppers are a great snack. Here is a recipe for pepper slices with filling from *The Joy of Cooking*. This famous cookbook, written by Irma S. Rombauer and Marion Rombauer Becker, was first published in 1931. It's still a favorite among cooks. Ingredients followed by an asterisk are optional.

2 medium green or red peppers
1 3-ounce (85-g) package of cream cheese
1 tablespoon (15 ml) cream or milk
1 teaspoon chopped onion or chives*
1 tablespoon (15 ml) lemon or lime juice*
1 tablespoon finely chopped celery*
¼ cup chopped stuffed green olives*
3 tablespoons chopped crisp bacon*

Core and seed green or red bell peppers. Set aside. Combine the cream cheese with milk or cream. Mash until soft. Add one or more of the optional ingredients. Stuff the peppers with the cream cheese. Chill for 12 hours. Slice each pepper into 4 to 6 pieces using a sharp knife dipped in hot water.

PREPARING THE GARDEN FOR WINTER

Even though your garden may be resting in fall and winter, there are plenty of things to keep you busy. After harvest, clean up around your garden. Pick up any fruits or vegetables that may have fallen to the ground and put them in your compost or discard them.

You may plant rye grass or buckwheat in your garden space to prevent erosion and provide nutrients for your soil. This is also a good time to spread compost or manure over the garden.

Clean and store your garden tools. They will last longer if you put them away until you need them again. Start planning for next year. Think about your garden plan. What worked and what didn't? Sketch out a new plan while these ideas are fresh in your mind. Make notes on your favorite flowers and vegetables and on those you didn't like. In late winter, start going through catalogs and making lists of what you want to buy to plant.

Taking care of your compost is a year-round job. Don't forget to turn it occasionally and keep

Not all vegetables get picked at the same time. Lettuces can be picked throughout the growing season as they appear. Peppers can be picked early, when they're still yellow or green, or late, when they start to turn bright orange or red.

it moist (except when it's frozen hard). It will reward you in the spring at planting time.

PLANTING A FALL CROP

Quite a few vegetables grow well in cool weather. Lettuce, broccoli, brussels sprouts, kale, collards, and mustard and turnip greens are favorite fall plants. They can even tolerate snow and light freezes. For many gardeners, late August and September are exciting, not only because harvest is in full swing but also because they can plant more good things to eat.

The planting methods for fall crops are the same as for summer ones. It is important to check the "days to maturity" for what you plant to make sure you are allowing enough time for the plants to reach harvest before hard winter sets in.

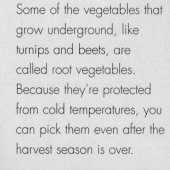

Some of the vegetables that grow underground, like turnips and beets, are called root vegetables. Because they're protected from cold temperatures, you can pick them even after the harvest season is over.

CHAPTER 6
SPECIAL GARDENS

GARDENS FOR BIRDS, BUTTERFLIES, AND BEES

A vegetable garden is only one of many types of gardens. Many gardeners grow plants to give butterflies, hummingbirds, bats, or other creatures a place to gather and eat. Watching what comes and goes in the garden is the gardener's reward. They spend time on warm afternoons and at dusk watching wild visitors. They often keep lists of the kinds of creatures they see in their backyards.

To attract birds, bees, butterflies, and bats, gardeners plant almonds, apples, blueberries, cherries, cucumbers, pumpkins, and zucchini—a few of the plants that rely on pollinators. Native plants that need pollinators include asters, coneflowers, snapdragons, saguaro, and yuccas. You might be surprised by the other critters that these plants may attract. Depending on where you live, you might see opossums, deer, raccoons, and rabbits.

The future of our farms depends on pollinators. About 80 percent of the crops that feed people around the world are pollinated by wild bees and other wildlife. The other 20 percent are pollinated by honeybees. But honeybees are in decline.

Corn probably originated in Mexico and Central America. It wasn't long before Native Americans in what would later become the United States were planting it, too.

Diseases, pesticides, and Africanized honeybees are the main causes. In the wild, many native bees, birds, bats, and other pollinators are threatened by pesticides and loss of habitat. Few people understand how much we depend on pollinators. Without them, farmers would not be able to feed the six billion people on the planet.

A world full of pollinators is a world full of diversity. Scientists estimate that at least 100,000 species of insects, birds, and mammals pollinate 250,000 kinds of plants. By helping plants reproduce, pollinators are like little machines that drive biological diversity on our planet. Fewer pollinators mean fewer plants.

A NATIVE AMERICAN GARDEN

Gardens have long been places for Native Americans to gather. While they tended plants, the gardeners talked. In her book *Brother Crow, Sister Corn,* Carol Buchanan writes about how Iroquois women formed the Good Rule Society. Their goals were to take care of the gardens and to care for old and sick people in the tribe. Buchanan also tells about the Mandan and the Hidatsa, who formed the Goose Woman Society. Their goal was to take care of the crops, especially the corn, that nourished their families.

For many Native Americans, gardening is part of their spiritual life. They have rituals for planting, harvesting, and protecting crops from drought and pests. The story of a tribe's beginnings on the earth is often about a native plant, usually corn. The Yuma's origin story is about Kakh, Brother Crow, who brought Sister Corn, who gives her life to the people.

Learning about Native American gardening ceremonies helps us to respect the cultures

and religions of other people. These stories, songs, and rituals remind us how important food is to everyone's survival.

Three Sisters Garden

The name Haudenosaunee means "People of the Long-house" and is the collective name of a group of five Native American nations. The nations are the Mohawk, the Oneida, the Onondaga, the Cayuga, and the Seneca. These peoples lived in what would become the northeastern United States. The group is also known as the Iroquois.

The Haudenosaunee peoples, like many Native Americans, grew corn, beans, and squash. It is thought that the Haudenosaunee began the tradition of calling these plants the Three Sisters. As the Onondaga chief Louis Farmer said, "So long as the Three Sisters are with us we know we will never starve."

The Three Sisters are good companions. In the book *Native American Gardening*, Michael Caduto and Joseph Bruchac explain why corn, beans, and squash grow so well together. The cornstalk provides good support for the bean vines. The bacteria on the beans' roots produce nitrogen. The nitrogen fertilizes the corn and squash. Squash, which is a sprawling plant with big leaves, helps control soil erosion. Also, weeds have trouble growing in the shade of the squash plants.

NATIVE SEEDS

In the 1980s, people of the Tohono O'odham tribe living in the desert near Tucson, Arizona, began to look for seeds for traditional crops. Their ancestors had developed plants to grow in the hot, dry climate, but it was getting hard to find the old varieties. The Tohono O'odham people realized they might lose part of their cultural heritage forever.

Native Seeds/SEARCH was organized in 1983 to help the Tohono O'odham find their seeds. From this beginning, the group has become a major seed bank for rare heirlooms and now has more than 4,600 members.

Learning from Native American Gardens

Climate still limits what gardeners can grow, but most gardeners now have access to water. Many people have forgotten that as recently as the early 1900s, gardeners had to use their wits to grow plants in the semiarid and arid parts of the world. They knew how to hoard every drop of water. Their knowledge is being lost.

The word Wampanoag translates as "People of the First Light." These people are the Native Americans who helped save the Pilgrims from starvation after they landed on the North American continent in 1620.

The Wampanoag plant corn and beans on mounds of dirt. The circular mounds measure 4 inches (10 cm) high and 18 inches (46 cm) wide. The Wampanoag hollow out a shallow depression about 10 inches (25 cm) wide in the top of the mound. The depression holds water like a saucer. Four corn seeds are planted in the saucer-shaped top of the mound.

After the corn plants are about 4 inches (10 cm) high, four bean seeds are planted on the slope of the mound. It is an important part of the Wampanoag ceremony to plant the corn and bean seeds at the four points of the compass—that is, north, south, east, and west.

In the deserts of southwestern North America, only 6 or 7 inches (15 to 18 cm) of rain fall each year. The Hopi build waist-high rock terraces on the slopes of hills or mesas where water emerges from a spring or seep. In this way, they can capture rain as it percolates through the soil or drains down the slope of the hill.

Zuni waffle gardens are designed to conserve precious water in the desert. The Zuni build a berm, or low wall, of soil about 5 inches (13 cm) high to form a rectangular plot. They plant several seeds from a variety of crops in each plot.

The size of the plot is typically never bigger than 4 feet (1.2 m) on a side. This allows a gardener to easily reach all the plants growing in the plot. The Zuni fill each plot with water, and the berm holds and concentrates the water like a saucer. No drop of water is wasted. A cluster of Zuni gardens looks just like a big waffle.

GARDENING WITH YOUR COMMUNITY

What brings people together to garden? Often it is hard times. People cannot afford to buy food—or there is no food to buy. In 1894, during an economic depression in the United States, the mayor of Detroit allowed more than nine hundred families to grow food in garden plots on 455 acres (184 hectares) of land in the city. Other major cities began similar programs. As the economy improved, most of the gardens vanished. During times of peace and prosperity, it is hard to imagine the powerful force of necessity.

During World War I and World War II, canned goods, gasoline, and other products were rationed in the United States. The government urged people to plant victory gardens in their backyards and communities. The response was overwhelming. During World War II, twenty million Americans worked in victory gardens and raised 40 percent of the country's food. In part, the victory gardens provided food for everyone to eat. But the gardens also helped people come together and support each other during wartime.

With peace and prosperity, most people abandoned their victory gardens. But a few have remained. The Richard Parker Memorial Victory Garden, run by the Fenway Garden Society in Boston, began in 1944 and is still going. It is one of the largest community gardens in the country. There are more than five hundred plots and many activity areas, including a children's garden, Japanese garden, and special needs garden.

Since the 1960s and 1970s, there has been a growing interest in community gardens. More people want to eat food

During World War II (1939–1945), people in the United States planted victory gardens. Here, Girl Scouts in wartime California learn how to plant seedlings in the soil.

grown without pesticides. They want to know where their food comes from. They want to take an active part in growing fresh, healthy food. Between 1995 and 2000, the number of community gardens in the United States increased by 22 percent. In 1998 the American Community Garden Association determined there were 6,020 community gardens nationwide tended by two million gardeners. In 2000 there were 1,906 community gardens in New York City alone!

A community garden can provide food for low-income families or be a place where children can gather in summer to learn new skills. In her book *A Patch of Eden: America's Inner City Gardeners*, Patricia Hynes writes about people in big cities across the United States who are using gardens to make their communities better, safer, and happier places to live. One garden can feed the minds, bodies, and spirits of many people.

Caring for each other is one reason why the U.S. Department of Agriculture is bringing back the idea of the victory garden. It is asking people to

plant gardens—at home, at school, and in their communities. The program is called Millennium Gardens, in celebration of the new millennium.

Millennium gardeners agree to share. They can give a portion of their produce to a local food bank or share flowers with hospitals and nursing homes. They agree to practice garden methods that protect the soil and water in their communities. The Millennium Gardens program proves that people don't need hard times or war to have a reason to plant gardens. Caring for our communities is reason enough.

In Chicago, Illinois, kids work together to haul dirt for a community flower garden.

Mail-Order
SEEDS AND SUPPLIES

The Cook's Garden
P.O. Box 535
Londonderry, VT 05148
<http://www.cooksgarden.com>

Johnny's Selected Seeds
230 Foss Hill Road
Albion, ME 04910-9731
<http://www.johnnyseeds.com>

Park Seed Co.
P.O. Box 46
Cokesbury Road
Greenwood, SC 29648-0046
<http://www.parkseed.com>

Seed Savers Exchange
Send $1 to:
Seed Savers Exchange
3076 North Winn Road
Decorah, IA 52101

Shepherd's Garden Seeds
30 Irene Street
Torrington, CT 06790
<http://www.shepherdseeds.com>

W. Atlee Burpee Garden
300 Park Avenue
Warminster, PA 18974
<http://www.burpee.com>

WEB HELP

Bat ecology and conservation
<http://www.batcon.org>

Community gardens
<http://www.communitygarden.org>
<http://www.gardenfutures.org>

Farmers' markets
<http://www.ams.usda.gov/farmersmarkets>

General gardening information
<http://www.gardenersnet.com>
<http://www.gardenguides.com>
<http://www.gardening.com>
<http://www.greenthumbgoodies.com>
  <http://www.thevegetablepatch.com>
  <http://www.yourgarden.com>

Millennium Gardens
<http://www.millenniumgreen.usda.gov>

Native American information
<http://www.nativeweb.com>

Native heirloom seeds
<http://www.azstarnet.com/~nss>

Native plants
<http://www.wildflowers.avatartech.com>

Pollinators
<http://www.desertmusuem.org/fp>

Wild lawns
<http://www.for-wild.org>
<http://www.nwf.org/habitats>
<http://www.prairienursery.org.>
<http://www.wildflowerfarm.com>

BOOK HELP

Backyard Composting: Your Complete Guide to Recycling Yard Clippings. Sebastopol, CA: Harmonious Press, 1997.

Barton, Barbara. *Gardening by Mail*. Boston: Houghton Mifflin, 1997.

Boring, John Kadel, et al. *Natural Gardening*. New York: The Nature Company/Time Life Books, 1995.

Brennan, Georgeanne, and Ethel Brennan. *The Children's Kitchen Garden: A Book of Gardening, Cooking, and Learning*. Berkeley, CA: Ten Speed Press, 1997.

Buchanan, Carol. *Brother Crow, Sister Corn: Traditional American Indian Gardening*. Berkeley, CA: Ten Speed Press, 1997.

Caduto, Michael J., and Joseph Bruchac. *Native American Gardening: Stories, Projects and Recipes for Families*. Golden, CO: Fulcrum Publishing, 1996.

Campbell, Stu. *Let It Rot!: The Gardener's Guide to Composting*. Pownal, VT: Storey Communications, 1998.

Christopher, Tom, and Marty Asher. *Compost This Book!* San Francisco, CA: Sierra Club Books, 1994.

Coleman, Eliot. *The New Organic Grower*. 2nd ed. White River Junction, VT: Chelsea Green Publishing Co., 1995.

Cox, Jeff. *Your Organic Garden*. Emmaus, PA: Rodale Press, 1994.

Glassberg, Jeffrey. *Butterflies through Binoculars: The East*. New York: Oxford University Press, 1999.

Hessayon, D. G. *The Container Expert*. London: Expert Books, Transworld Publishers Ltd., 1997.

Hynes, H. Patricia. *A Patch of Eden: America's Inner City Gardeners*. White River Junction, VT: Chelsea Green Publishing Co., 1996.

King, John. *Reaching for the Sun: How Plants Work*. New York: Cambridge University Press, 1997.

Kite, L. Patricia. *Garden Wizardry for Kids*. Hauppauge, NY: Barron's, 1995.

Meltzer, Milton. *The Amazing Potato*. New York: HarperCollins, 1992.

Natural Insect Control: The Ecological Gardener's Guide to Foiling Pests. Brooklyn Botanic Garden 21st-Century Gardening Series, Handbook #139. Brooklyn, NY, 1999.

Richardson, Beth. *Gardening with Children*. Newtown, CT: Taunton Press, 1998.

Stell, Elizabeth P. *Secrets to Great Soil*. Pownal, VT: Storey Communications, 1998.

Strickland, Sue. *Heirloom Vegetables: A Home Gardener's Guide to Finding and Growing Vegetables from the Past*. New York: Fireside, 1998.

Stuckey, Maggie. *Gardening from the Ground Up*. New York: St. Martin's Press, 1998.

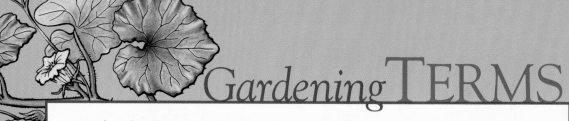

Gardening TERMS

annual: a plant that germinates, flowers, produces fruit, and dies within one season

climate: the usual pattern of weather of a particular region. The average temperature, amount of rainfall or other precipitation, and wind combine to create climate.

compost: decayed organic matter—often consisting of grass clippings, leaves, and vegetable peels—used to improve the soil in the garden

heirloom plant: a plant selected for a particular trait or set of traits. It may be crossbred to enhance the desirable traits.

hybrid plant: a plant created when two different species or varieties of plants are crossbred. Crossbreeding allows scientists to develop disease-resistant plants that grow bigger fruits.

mulch: the organic or inorganic material layered on the soil around plants to control weeds or keep in moisture

native plant: a plant that originated in a particular climate or landscape and that has not been genetically altered

nutrient: a substance used as food by plants or animals

organic gardening: a way of growing food or flowers in which chemicals are not used to control pests or to fertilize crops

organic matter: material from any living thing. Organic matter also contains billions of creatures, such as bacteria, that maintain the soil's health.

perennial: a plant that sprouts, grows, and produces flowers or fruits every year for many years

photosynthesis: the process by which green plants use sunlight to create food from carbon dioxide, minerals, and water

potential hydrogen (pH): a scale measuring the number of hydrogen ions in soil. An ion is an atom or molecule with a positive or negative electric charge. The number of hydrogen ions determines how nutrients are absorbed.

Gardens to VISIT

Brooklyn Botanic Garden
100 Washington Avenue
Brooklyn, NY 11225
<http://www.bbg.org>
Has excellent programs, including the Discovery Garden, where kids and adults can touch, smell, and hear plants

Denver Botanic Gardens
1005 York Street
Denver, CO 80206
<http://www.botanicgardens.org>
Features the Children's Secret Path, with tunnels, mazes, and other surprises

Fairchild Tropical Garden
10901 Old Cutler Road
Coral Gables, FL 33156
<http://www.ftg.org>
The largest tropical garden in the continental United States

The Huntington Botanical Gardens
1151 Oxford Road
San Marino, CA 91108
<http://www.huntington.org>
Features overnight theme-based adventures and workshops on creating bonsai trees, making paper, and arranging flowers

Longwood Gardens
U.S. Route 1
P. O. Box 501
Kennett Square, PA 19348
<http://www.longwoodgardens.org>
Features indoor and outdoor plant trails that highlight fall foliage and when to plant spring bulbs

Minnesota Landscape Arboretum
3675 Arboretum Drive
P. O. Box 39
Chanhassen, MN 55317
<http://www.arboretum.umn.edu>
Walks on the Wild Side visit prairies, woodlands, and bogs, and a motorized tram takes visitors on a 3-mile (5-km) tour

Missouri Botanical Garden
4344 Shaw Boulevard
St. Louis, MO 63110
<http://www.mgbnet.mobot.org>
<http://www.mobot.org>
(great website for kids!)
Excellent programs include Summer Science Academy, Youth EcoCorps, and activities for homeschooling

Norfolk Botanical Gardens
6700 Azalea Garden Road
Norfolk, VA 25318
<http://www.virginiagarden.org>
Has varied activities, including egg hunts, twenty theme gardens (including children's gardens), historical reenactments, workshops, and day camps

San Antonio Botanical Gardens
555 Funston Place
San Antonio, TX 78209
<http://www.sabot.org>
(Check out Maja's Rainforest!)
Highly successful kids' programs include working with expert gardeners, building your own terrarium, and gardening for self-sufficiency

Washington Park Arboretum
University of Washington
2300 Arboretum Drive East
P. O. Box 358010
Seattle, WA 98112
<http://depts.washington.edu/wpa/>
Free arboretum features school-oriented tours on plant life cycles, native plants of the area, and wetland management

INDEX

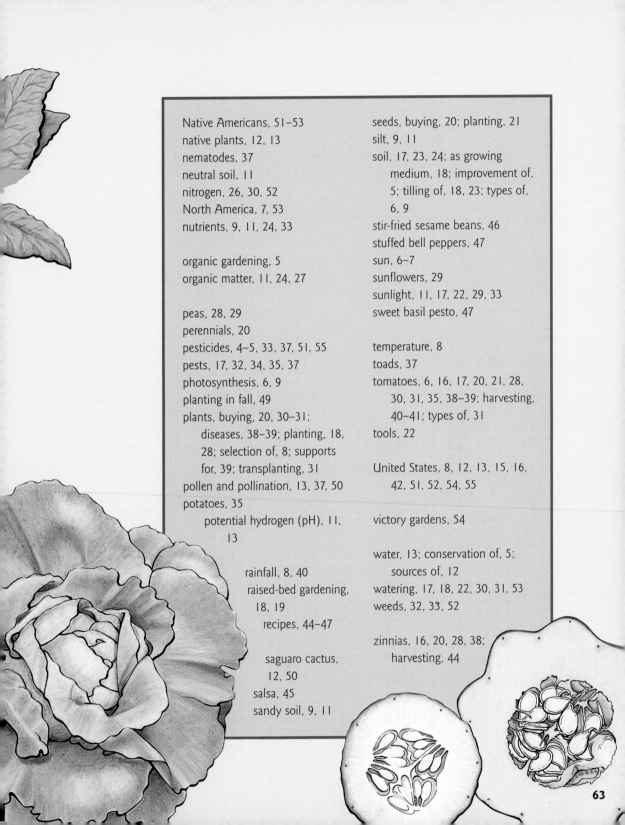

ABOUT THE AUTHOR

Suzanne Winckler has written about nature and the environment for twenty years. These pursuits led her to gardening and an interest in sustainable agriculture and livestock husbandry. With mentoring from David F. Smith, her husband and longtime gardener, she has tilled, mulched, weeded, and maintained composts in Minnesota, Nebraska, and Arizona.

ACKNOWLEDGMENTS

The photographs in this book are reproduced courtesy of: Todd Strand/Independent Picture Service, pp. 1, 2-3, 8, 21, 22, 23, 28, 59, 60; USDA Photo, pp. 9, 20, 27, 49 (left), 55; © Robert Perron, p. 15; © Karlene V. Schwartz, pp. 17, 19, 33, 44, 50; Trinity Muller/Independent Picture Service, pp. 24, 39; © Jack K. Clark/AGStockUSA, pp. 34, 35, 36; © Scott Sinklier/ AGStockUSA, p. 43; Jim Simondet/Independent Picture Service, p. 48; Steve Foley/Independent Picture Service, p. 49 (right); Tennessee State Museum, detail of a painting by Carlyle Urello, p. 51; Franklin D. Roosevelt Library, [NLR-PHOCO-66298(8)], p.54.

Cover: photos by Todd Strand/Independent Picture Service; illustrations by Laura Westlund.

The illustrations on pages 1, 2, 4, 6, 7, 10, 12, 14, 28, 30, 31, 40, 41, 42, 45, 46, 52, 56-57, 58-59, 60, 61, 62-63, 64 are by Laura Westlund.